# Robbie Learns a Lesson on Truth

~Sardines~

Karen Vincent
Illustrated by Glenda Bowlin

AuthorHouse™
1663 Liberty Drive
Bloomington, IN 47403
www.authorhouse.com
Phone: 833-262-8899

Because of the dynamic nature of the Internet, any web addresses or links contained in this book may have changed since publication and may no longer be valid. The views expressed in this work are solely those of the author and do not necessarily reflect the views of the publisher, and the publisher hereby disclaims any responsibility for them.

This book is printed on acid-free paper.

ISBN: 978-1-4490-5772-5 (sc)

Print information available on the last page.

Published by AuthorHouse  03/19/2021

authorHOUSE

This book is dedicated to my husband, Bill, and my daughters, Kim and Teri, for all their encouragement. Also to my seven grandchildren, whom I hope enjoy reading the book as much as I enjoyed writing it.

A mouse named Robbie loved to scamper around the house after everyone else had gone to bed. He knew his parents didn't want him to go downstairs, but his curiosity always got the better of him. Besides, he always brought sweets to share with his twin brother, Bobbie, who shared a room with him in the attic.

Robbie always tried to get his twin, Bobbie, to go downstairs with him, but Bobbie said he wasn't curious and didn't want any trouble. Of course, he certainly didn't mind eating the sweets, especially the cake, cookie crumbs, and strawberries that Robbie brought back. In fact, he was getting a little chubby from eating so much and doing so little.

Robbie's father, Doug, his mother, Martha, and his twin brother, Bobbie, had always lived at the Murphys' house. They were very clean mice and never left droppings around to alert anyone that they were there. They loved living in this beautiful house, mainly because there was no cat and the Murphys never set traps.

One night it was nearly midnight before everyone had gone to bed. There had been lots of people at the Murphys' home. They had a birthday party for their son, Timmy, earlier in the day. Mr. and Mrs. Murphy stayed up late cleaning up the dishes from the party. They decided they would just do the dishes and leave the rest of the mess until morning.

When Robbie got downstairs this night he watched as street mice came out of every nook and cranny.

Robbie hadn't counted on the extra mice that had come from the streets around the Murphy house. They were helping themselves to the leftover birthday cake, cheese and crackers, lunch meat, and bread crumbs from the sandwiches. The leftovers were scattered all over the cabinets, table, and floor. All Robbie managed to get was a little crumb of birthday cake that had been flung behind the cabinet. These leftovers had always belonged to the mouse family.

*Oh dear*, he thought to himself, *this is the biggest mess I've ever seen.* When the mouse family cleaned up the leftovers they also cleaned up the napkins, wrapping paper, and balloons, and they also washed up the cabinets and table until they were shining. Robbie knew he had to get this cleaned up by morning, before the Murphy family got up to go to work. He would have to enlist some help. This job was way too big for one mouse. He thought of getting Bobbie to help, but knew he'd grumble and be too slow anyway.

"Dear God" he prayed, "please tell me what to do. If I go to my parents, they'll be mad at me because I sneaked out so late. If I don't tell them, though, the Murphys might get a cat or set out a bunch of traps." Then Robbie remembered something his father had read from the old Bible they had retrieved from the attic "The truth will set you free."

He loved that his father read the Bible to him, because it always came in handy when he needed help or comfort. Having the Word in his heart was like having Jesus with him always.

Without a moment's hesitation, he ran upstairs and woke up his parents. He told them what had happened. They were not even mad, because he'd done the right thing by telling the truth. His parents hurried and woke up Bobbie, and of course he grumbled, but he did go with them.

By the time they got to the kitchen, all the stray mice had gone back to the streets, where they lived in trash cans. Some of them lived with the homeless people, where they might pick up a crumb or two.

Robbie and his family, with their little broom and dust pan, put bits of wrapping paper, balloons, napkins, and yucky mouse dropping into baggies. As each baggie was filled, Robbie would swing up onto the cabinet and drop it in the waste basket.

They dragged themselves back upstairs just as they heard Mrs. Murphy yawning from her bedroom. They knew she was getting ready to go to the kitchen to make coffee. Robbie and his family made their way to their little box beds in the attic, Doug said to Robbie rather sternly, "We are very glad you told us the truth about tonight.

As you know it says in the Bible that the truth will set you free, but you could have been hurt by those street mice." Secretly they were thankful he had gone downstairs that night of all nights. They knew, as Robbie did, what the consequences would have been if he hadn't seen the street mice. Poor Bobbie, with his fat little belly hitting each stair step along the way, was still making his way to bed and grumbling more than ever.

All of them were nearly asleep before their heads hit their pillows. They slept the rest of the day.

~Sardines~

Printed in the United States
by Baker & Taylor Publisher Services